Made in the USA
Coppell, TX
03 March 2020

16453821R00057